HISPANIC GAME

de la Riva group
USA
A KITELAB COMPANY

PUBLISHED BY DE LA RIVA GROUP/KITELAB USA LLC
5805 Blue Lagoon Drive, Suite 135
Miami, FL 33126

EDITORIAL PROJECT BY **PE&A**
EDITED BY **ELVIA NAVARRO JURADO**
DESIGNED BY **ANDRÉS GÓMEZ SERVÍN**
TRANSLATED BY **HARRY PORTER**
PROOFREADING BY **LISA HELLER**

ISBN **978-607-9121-02-0**

HISPANIC GAME

CARLOS DE LEON DE LA RIVA
PRISCILA ARAMBURU MENA
ADELINA VACA PADILLA

de la Riva group
USA
A KITELAB COMPANY

INtroduducTioN

From the outset, we've been the kind of research agency that loves finding out why things happen. So although it seemed preposterous to produce yet more knowledge about the Hispanic market (you might even be thinking, "Please, enough already!"), we decided to roll up our sleeves and dig into the lives of these people, because we thought we could shed even clearer light on their story.

We developed a syndicated intuitive study with anthropological and quantitative methodologies that would take us inside Hispanic life. We were in their homes, we were at their table with them, we drank with them, we played with their children, worked on farms and in offices with them, pulled double shifts, visited with their families back in the home country and added more than a few to our Facebook and follow them on Twitter. We even cleaned some of their houses. We spared no efforts in finding out what it means to be Hispanic in the United States.

We wondered why we sometimes take for granted that being Hispanic means having different cultural characteristics, special needs even, from the rest of the population. Although it is part of the truth, we further discovered Hispanics shape themselves and understand each other in relation to the value they are able to contribute to the host culture.

This is why we went past the cultural differences to find what motivated Hispanics' decisions and to know what they are questing for. At one time, women were in a similar situation. They shared a mission to liberate themselves, and many of their life decisions had to do with it (hence, they bought more practical products, dedicated more time to themselves, went to work, etc.). In those days, women were united, not just due to gender, but because, together, they could make common cause. Today, what Hispanics are striving for goes beyond cultural elements; it has to do with furnishing value and shaping an identity while forever playing and trying on identities.

In this context, we want to let you know that our study started out like a blank canvas on which Hispanics expressed their feelings about themselves and the world around them. We wanted the findings gathered by this project to faithfully portray the Hispanic point of view. We let them say whatever they wanted, and with their accounts, we put together this book you are about to read.

WHERE DOES THE INFORMATION IN THIS BOOK COME FROM?

What you will discover in this book is a summary of the findings gathered through a broad market study of a syndicated nature.

De la Riva-Kitelab Syndicated Studies not only monitor data: they help to delve into what gives meaning to people's lives, how they construct their identity, experience social dynamics and the market potential they represent. They are tools for a more in-depth reading of the market. They are knowledge, inspiration, culture and even personal curiosity. They are platforms of insights that connect our clients' world with the consumer beyond categories.

OUR ANTHROPOLOGICAL APPROACH

We used the family as a research unit. We talked with all the members, and all their perspectives went into piecing the story together. We were able to contextualize each one of their stories. We met their friends and extended family, their companions and even their enemies. We lived with them for 90 days!

We visited with the families of the Hispanos in their countries of origin. They showed us photos and told us what it means to have family in the United States. We also chatted with Hispanics that had returned home after being in the U.S. for years, and they told us what they missed from "up yonder."

We have over 540 hours on film and tape. Some of the Hispanics took over the camera and directed their own movie. We took snapshots, kids did drawings of us and teenagers made up song lists for us.

We talked with a lot of non-Hispanics: Anglos, African Americans, Koreans, Iranians, Polish people, Italians... All of them helped us explain what Hispanics are like and the kind of relationship they have with them. Taxi drivers and bartenders were certainly our great allies.

We don't pretend to delve into a theoretical discussion with it nor debate about the authors who have contributed valuable road maps for understanding the huge minority that makes up the Hispanic market. Neither is it our intention to compile memoirs and anecdotes in the raw or put out a cute photo album. What you will find, though, is the story Hispanics tell about themselves. A spotlight onto how they play their life's chess pieces and how this game effects the majority of their behaviors.

When you come to the end of the book, the experience will have afforded you a feeling for the meaning of living day-by-day as a Hispanic in the United States. Above all, you will have found elements, themes, stories and excuses to strike up a conversation with them, whether as a professional, brand, researcher, vendor, product, strategist, publicist or just a regular person.

We let you know the ins and outs of the Hispanic game so you can decide how your brand, strategy or communication can play, too.

TECHNICAL SPECIFICATION
FOR THE STUDY

ANTHROPOLOGICAL PHASE

WHO

First, second and third generation Hispanics, ages 18-50, of all
economic statuses and hailing from various Latin American countr

WHERE

Los Angeles, Chicago, New York, Houston and Miami

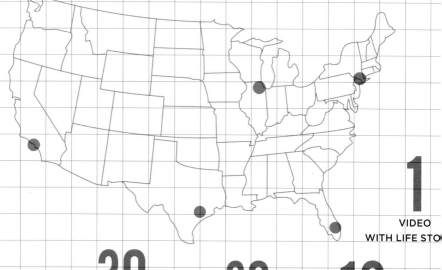

1 VIDEO WITH LIFE STO

HOW MANY **30** ETHNOGRAPHIC FAMILY IMMERSIONS

30 ON-SITE FOCUS GROUPS

12 PUBLIC ETHNOGRAPHIES

like to address different questions with different methodologies. do so, we created a dynamic design that brought in an anthropological proach and closed with a quantitative phase. Here's how we did it.

UANTITATIVE PHASE

HO

rst, second and third generation Hispanics, ages 18-50, of all onomic statuses and hailing from various Latin American countries

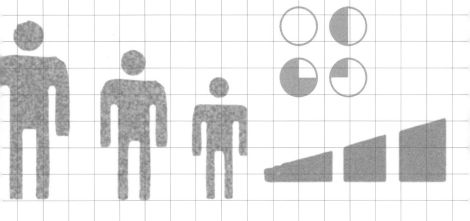

HERE

ationwide

OW MANY

1,900

INTERVIEWS

SEMI-STRUCTURED
QUESTIONNAIRES
THAT INTERVIEWEES COULD
ANSWER IN EITHER ENGLISH
OR SPANISH

chapter

ter 1

The **Two** FOLD

HISPANIC QUEST:

BREAKING **Out** of the Stereo-type

AND

VALIDATION

dlR
de la Riva group

Hispanics refer to themselves by this term not because they feel it's fitting but because it is a mutually agreed-upon grouping label. What's more, it makes everybody's job easier. However, to assume that this concept conveys a clear reading of identity would be a mistake, and to think we can rely on it to map out communication strategies is to further err.

The fact that people say they are Hispanic denotes nothing more than acceptance of a label they generally feel constrained to use. Furthermore, the rather ambiguous term "Hispanic" has branched off into further stereotyping expressions such as "beaner" or "whitewashed". As seen below, both accentuate identity clichés:

BEANER

SEEKS TO STAY APART
PATRIOTIC TOWARD THE HOMELAND
SOCIALIZES EXCLUSIVELY WITHIN THE GROUP
LOW EDUCATION ASPIRATIONS
FLAUNTS THE LAW

WHITEWASHED

SEEKS TO MIMIC
PATRIOTIC TOWARD THE USA
SOCIALIZES OUTSIDE THE GROUP
ASPIRES TO EDUCATION
ABIDES BY THE LAW

Flaws Hispanics perceive in themselves, ignorance for starters, fuel the stereotyp

Hispanics shun both stereotypes, whether the lazy, ignorant one that flaunts the law or the one whose portrayal of the all-American falls short. And in their efforts to distance themselves from either extreme, they risk falling into the clutches of the other, which makes avoiding being stereotyped a rather complex experience.

The same can happen with brands. The pursuit of authenticating themselves as thoroughly Hispanic is at times so fervent that they resort to superficial folklore (loud colors, emblems, customs), thus striking a discordant note in the community. At the other extreme, brands try so desperately to steer clear of Hispanic attributes, despite these being an inherent component of their essence that they transform into American wannabes, speciously copying or misconstruing symbols. At the folkloric extreme, let's imagine a typical Mexican alcoholic beverage that attempts to get its message out to first-generation Hispanics by playing up the stereotypical image of a festive, boozy Mexican and is subsequently rebuffed by the target generation and all others as well.

Thus Hispanic, whether term or idea, rather than portraying an identity, has become a concept running between disparate stereotypes that is very distant from what the community truly feels and likes. Does this mean we can't use the term? Of course neither they nor we will stop using it anytime soon. It's simply a wake-up call that we need to take into account each individual's very own, differentiated and cherished self, regardless of the group name.

Because they feel society at large questions their standing, Hispanics are constantly searching for the means, viewpoints and brands that can aid them in constructing an identity that makes them worthy in the eyes of others. In other words, they endeavor to demonstrate they have something to contribute, as Hispanics constantly have to validate themselves to others and demonstrate that their presence in the United States is meaningful.

This phenomenon is comparable to a recently hired professional. Doesn't he need to justify his being hired, at the very least for a three-month period? Won't he have to show he's a complement to the company, especially if he landed a good job? Hispanics undergo the same thing, but without let-up and almost habitually. They are constantly confronted with dilemmas as to which customs, brands or attitudes will best serve to validate them, while the labels and the immigration system insist on reminding them they belong to a group apart that is not true-blue American.

Basically, there are two avenues of approach for Hispanic validation, one heading toward the country of origin, the other the United States. On the first, validation comes with their ability to extend the American Dream's values such as economic and educational success into the country of origin while the second, oriented toward the U.S., involves contributing extra value to the host society that questions them.

AV. 1: VALIDATION IN THE COUNTRY OF ORIGIN OR HERITAGE

Naturally, achieving validation in the country of origin and in the United States differs considerably. Some decide to migrate not solely for economic reasons or due to pressing hardships in their home countries, but rather to uphold a now long-established custom.

For example, in our study, which includes the families "that stayed behind", we discovered there is a tradition-related cause to migrate. In the words of these families, "Everybody has to let someone go." Many migrants come in order to carry out a sort of ritual among their relatives and their communities, by which they undergo a total transformation in terms of status, role, moral authority and power of decision in the hometown. Hence, beyond the economic benefits, the leave taking brings advantages to those that do it, as they stand to become opinion leaders back home. Their achievements go into constructing a superior personal image and to uplifting their family's image as well.

However, the weight of the migrant tradition and the expectations built into it (not just in terms of remittances, but for success in school, job and family life) even spill over into the generations born in the United States. One way or another, these people become vehicles for making these attainments tangible. The effort to justify leaving the homeland prevails in all generations of Hispanics. What better way does the first generation have to validate its success if not by having a daughter graduate from college? How could she, the second generation, fail to graduate if both she and her parents need this feather in their cap in order to validate themselves? It is precisely within the drive for validation that we discover trends that travel at lightening speed between the United States and Latin America. Let's look at the simple case of a first-generation Guatemalan who is sad because he's not home for Christmas. When he phones the family, though, he tells them about learning how to make an American-style Christmas turkey. He emails the recipe with instructions, along with a photo of him in the snow wearing a huge "designer" coat: in the background, a big pickup. "This is Christmas here!"

The above demonstrates the need of Hispanics to involve others in the American Dream by way of validating oneself to the homeland. The folks back home, meanwhile, become beneficiaries of the American Dream through a change in lifestyle. This can be seen most notably in their houses, which they remodel and enlarge with the dollars they receive. They build basements, attics, second stories and add on American-style decorative touches. Families with a member in the U.S. never seem to finish building and remodeling in their attempt to show the community they are getting along just fine. Never-ending building says abundance.

WHAT DO YOU THINK MAKES HISPANICS LOOK SUCCESSFUL BACK IN THE HOME COUNTRY?

54
UNIVERSITY
STUDIES

13
BUILDING A
HOUSE IN THE
HOME COUNTRY

22
SENDING MONEY
HOME

5
OTHER

6
DOESN'T
KNOW

**Aspiring to these forms of success
does not mean they are attained
(decidedly, not all study college).**

The ones left behind also acquire vehicles, home appliances and technology, thus projecting an image of modernity. This happens in other matters as well, eating habits, for instance. Hispanics keep their families current on brands, trends and practical ways of doing things and the good life, which they adopt as a sign of progress. All this contributes to a genuine authentication.

The communities learn to decipher the emigrants' successes or failures by way of the brands they send home as presents. Ultimately, these are symbols of success that make a statement about those who send them and also those who receive them. Communities constantly monitor the success or failure of migrants to the United States, with families usually aware of what the others are receiving and how these gifts compare with their own.

The role brands play in this dynamic is cardinal. The desire for validation is so strong among Hispanics that they want their brands to have real significance in Latin America. Buying a brand of clothing that is not very well known back home simply will not do. How can they validate themselves if the symbol falls short?

What's interesting about this phenomenon is that even though Hispanics seek out brands that are socially desirable in Latin America, they also point out others in fashion in the U.S. via photographs and conversations. The flow of narrative and brand building between Hispanics and their friends and families back home is an ongoing signifier-exchange circle. Consequently, brands that today lack clout in Latin America stand a chance of becoming popular, thanks to the validation motive.

This infers that the Hispanics' efforts to be valued in the homeland demonstrates opportunities only for brands with the potential to communicate economic success, family progress, trendiness or modernity. Nevertheless, there's also room for brands that Hispanics hang onto (or at least appreciate) that are tied in with certain traditions, values and customs.

In this case, validation can come by conserving feast days and celebrations, typical foods, religious icons, devotion to the mother and much more. It's important to maintain common codes (customs and traditions) that make them respected in Latin America, in addition to communing with the America Dream. The idea is for everybody to be able to participate in and benefit from the migration.

AV. 2: VALIDATION IN THE UNITED STATES

Although validating oneself back in the homeland might be selective or circumstantial in consequence to factors such as the seasons of the year, in the United States the process is non-stop. To illustrate this, consider Hispanic-related businesses that in their quest for legitimacy spotlight the fact that they are Hispanic. For example, if an advertising agency were to omit portraying itself as a professional team of Hispanic-market experts, why not hire any other agency?

The situation is the same for industries, services and individuals. Often Hispanic conduct is intensified, exalting the quality of work or jobs only they can perform or the festive nature of Hispanic social life. In relation to this, it is not only money matters that spur them to work more and better: the work ethic is also essential to distinguishing and validating themselves in the United States.

In this pursuit, they also might intensify American behavior patterns such as refusing to use Spanish and insisting on English only, overblown patriotism for the U.S.A. and being a stickler for the rules. Their painstaking compliance with the law and the American way originates not only from their notions of obedience and respect but also from their need to demonstrate their worth to the United States. In their view, those that respect and obey the laws have greater worth, especially in light of the reputation of the Hispanic as a person who does not meet obligations.

For Central Americans, the two-fold quest has to do with validating themselves in their own countries of origin (not in Mexico) as well as being valued contributors to U.S. society.

Hispanics of Cuban descent have unique political and historical reasons that justify their presence in the United States. Furthermore, the near impossibility of returning to the old country makes their integration process much smoother.

Exaggerating behavior patterns is a compensatory measure that gives Hispanics the illusion of validation; distinction even. The perfect example is a second-generation 24-year-old soldier of Mexican descent that we met doing fieldwork for our study. Freshly returned from Iraq, he and some friends went to a bar. He was having a beer when some

Anglo Americans came out with, "Hey, Messkin, why don't you go back where you came from?" Angered by the taunt, he waded into a brief bar skirmish with them. He reasons that, "I'm an American, and I've done my part for my country. I'm proud of my origins, but I'm not going to let them call into question my love for my country."

The need for validation can lead to emulations of behavior to the point of recurring to stereotype. Although the young man's enlistment in the armed forces is a source of pride for his family, his burning desire to belong to American society approaches the American wannabe stereotype.

Clearly, anybody can fall into exaggerated behavior, much like the child who, in seeking parental approval by making good grades, becomes obsessed with studying. Still, this is an extremely relevant factor in understanding a market that, despite its diversity and complexity, is unified by its quest for legitimacy.

Brands, whether American, Latin American or global, run the same risk of exaggeration. In addressing the Hispanic market they can fall into the trap of overstating their service, their communication, their channels and even their functional benefits. It's as though they were shouting, "Hey, amigo, this product is for you Hispanics!" This calls to mind Hispanic stores whose interiors, displays and products are so overwhelmingly targeted at the market that they force the community to intensify its purchases. Naturally, this results in them missing out on the chance to try other products and experiences.

Fortunately for all, Hispanics have found a means to balance these behaviors by way of a game between American and Hispanic possibilities. As we shall see in the next chapter, they've learned to grasp onto whatever best fits their situation.

HIGHLIGHTS

Although the label **"Hispanic"** is practical, it does not represent an identity

The problem with the label is its weight of stereotyping

At times, avoiding one stereotype leads to slipping into another

Hispanics quest for validation on two fronts: the homeland and the U.S.

In the U.S., validation comes by way of intensifying Hispanic and American behaviors

In the homeland, validation comes from extending the American Dream, while preserving the codes that clearly identify a Latin American

Hispanics make use of brands, products and services to aid them in the validation process

cHApter 2

THE Cultural Contrasts

As we have seen, even before they come to the United States, Hispanics are already tagged with a largely misleading label that's hard to live down and hard to get rid of. In this chapter, we examine the makeup of their identity and the changes that take place when confronted or contrasted with American culture.

The cultural contrasting begins, as does everything in this account, with the first generation. When an immigrant arrives in the United States and sees the streets, buys in the stores and makes personal contacts for the first time, a process begins that will continue for the rest of his life and pass on to the second generation.

The clear idea he forms of what it means to be an American will remain with him forever. At the same time, he begins forming a distinct idea of what it really means to be from the country he left behind.

As with any comparison, it can very easily turn into a judgment: some things are better, some worse. The process can be quite painful when they take stock of the poverty, corruption, uncleanliness and poor education in the homeland.

On the other hand, they idealize the festivities, the exalted figure of the mother and the unity of family and community back home. Tourists have somewhat similar experiences as they note the distinctions between the place they're visiting and where they're from such as the food, the architecture, the amount of pedestrian traffic and ways of greeting. Unfamiliar surroundings always invite comparisons.

What's important here is the change Hispanics undergo in relation to what comes from their country of origin. Brands from Latin America must be mindful that Hispanics are pickier shoppers than people who've not had the migrant experience. It's because they're constantly comparing!

Some first-generation Hispanics, tired of comparing, decide that one culture is not any better than the other, just different. But the decision doesn't free them from dilemma. To the contrary, now doubts set in as to why they immigrated in the first place, creating conflict with their children and grandchildren and even within themselves.

There's a saying among many that, "It wasn't I who crossed the border, the border crossed me," meaning the decision to

I had a lot of expectations when I got here...
They took me by highway to a complex of brick
buildings, and I was thinking: 'All that effort
and money to come from Colombia, and the
United States turns out to be the same.'
It took me months to get my bearings and get
to Manhattan. That's where you find out the
United States will never be like Colombia.

Hispanic man, age 42,
first generation Colombian, New York City

Dad, will you please just stop it!

Stop saying that Americans are ignorant.

We're not ignorant, maybe it's just arrogance.

I do believe that America is the best country.

After all, we're living here, right?

Hispanic man, age 27, second generation, Guatemalan descent, Los Angeles emigrate wasn't their responsibility, it was their fate: a way to not have to justify their coming to the U.S. On the other hand, the second and third generations, who are generally more Americanized, have an easier time dealing with the dilemma. For them, American culture is more appealing in lots of ways.

As you can see, the subject is rather complex, so much so in fact that even if they make efforts to disengage from comparing, it remains a perpetual filter that affects how they view matters.

Like many other elements, brands are caught in the middle of this process of making comparisons. Many of them, especially food items, try to position themselves by tapping into the nostalgia vein, playing up Hispanic traits in their packaging, communications and marketing and by stressing their "original" or regional use. A first-generation Hispanic might identify with this sort of discourse if he's feeling homesick and longing for his family. But if a brand doesn't stick to the rules of American culture, it loses credibility, and he will be ashamed to use it. If this happens, the brand will be doomed to use in instances when individuals wax nostalgic instead of being a family staple.

Our anthropologists witnessed some anomalies in the Hispanic world. For instance, one interviewee's refrigerator had Mexican beer prominently stocked, however, when he wasn't paying attention, his young son pointed to where he had an American brand hidden away. Many other items like *cajeta* (caramelized milk spread) and peanut butter or whisky and tequila can also be compared as to whether they are consumed in private or in public.

Within this constant contrasting, not even media content escapes being limited to almost secretive personal consumption. Mothers, for example, will automatically stop watching their Latin American soap opera and switch to channels like Home & Health or Discovery when their children's friends come over. They wouldn't feel the need to conceal their favorite show if they or their kids weren't uncomfortable with content that is incompatible and can't be shared with Americans.

At times, first generation immigrants of Mexican origin are attracted to the nostalgic appeal of certain Hispanic brands. Their children aren't, though, because their life experiences have no connection with it. The second generation prefers American brands that better address their own aspirations.

It seems like a conundrum, but it's not. If Hispanics live amidst people of varied backgrounds, they better contextualize differences and similarities between their own and the American culture and are less constrained by comparisons. On the other hand, if their contact with Americans is minimal, they compare more harshly, as the division of cultures stresses differences over similarities. Hispanics living in contact with other cultures tend to soften their comparisons and be more open.

A Mexican couple in Schenectady, New York had been taking free English classes every week with classmates hailing from several countries. When they became aware that the Mexicans tended to be louder than the rest, they softened their speech in public. In contrast, a Hispanic couple living in the Bronx had never gone to Manhattan, because when they were on the subway they felt all eyes were on them, which they construed as discrimination. They were unaware their loud cell-phone conversations were drawing the attention.

This is relevant because, for good or ill, some brands favor, even fuel, an opposition between the imaginary Hispanic culture and the American culture. On the other hand, there are brands that set up a dialog inclusive of the numerous cultures that make up the American spirit, not just two of them.

It is wise to keep in mind that the multicultural dynamic is part of the essence of the United States. Every culture is expected to make a worthy contribution to the others. For brands, this means finding a way to appeal equally to Hispanics as well as Americans of all stripes in such a way that the multicultural focus featuring Hispanic values in an impartial context helps in the validation process.

For sure, this is a much harder task than keeping to basic distinguishers like nostalgia, but it pays off, especially if Hispanic values are enhanced.

In order for a brand to take advantage of this means of contrasting, it primarily needs to understand what constitutes intercultural comparison and the way Hispanics go about it.

A huge amount of research has gone into the contrasts between cultures, but our study goes further, to focus on how Hispanics perceive and experience these cultural differences on a daily basis.

I'm worried because my agency is cutting back on personnel. If I lose my job, I'll lose my work visa and have to go back to Mexico. I get along fine with my boss and the rest of the staff, but here you never know... Friday, everybody goes out for beer, and come Monday they could call me into the office to tell me, 'We're letting you go'.

Hispanic woman, age 36
first generation Mexican, Chicago

If the menu says it comes with three peas, it comes with three peas. If your plate comes with two or four, you can complain and they bring you another, no problem.

Hispanic woman, age 28,
first generation Salvadorian, Houston

The cultural comparisons we've mentioned can be summed up in two basic contrasts or differences:

● Protective relationships versus relationships of equality
● Flexible systems versus rigid systems

In Latin American countries, relationships lean toward the vertical, authoritarian style, while in the United States, where equality is valued, they are more horizontal. This implies that the expectations of people in the two cultures regarding relationships with family, friends and the government are substantially different.

In Hispanic relationships, the power of authority protects those beneath it but also takes advantage of them. However, those protected don't question the authority's (be it father, teacher or brand) loyalty and concern; they expect it.

On the other hand, the American way doesn't extend or expect any individual's protection of another. This is the nature of a social organization centered on creating equality among citizens so that each one is his own keeper. For instance, the current children's rights movement is making certain family, and even other vertical relationships, more horizontal. Horizontality fosters equality in relationships as well as in opportunities. The price of this openness is that, if all are equal, it follows that everyone must be responsible for himself.

Having left a protective society behind, Hispanics can feel forsaken in a system that values work and effort over personal relations and patronage, no matter the generation. In compensation, they set up job and protection networks with their contacts. To illustrate, many Miami taxi drivers, if unable to tend to a potential customer, will pass the client along to a Hispanic colleague. Although the custom of protection has its advantages, its dark side emerges when the protector requires loyalty and gratitude in exchange.

Nevertheless, Hispanics are pleasantly surprised to find out that in the United States they can express a complaint to a brand or service without it being taken personally. Not infrequently, you'll hear new arrivals exclaiming happily, "Here you can return defective purchases and no hard feelings." Naturally, they quickly grow accustomed to this egalitarian relationship with their brands and services and no longer stand for hitches in, for instance, cable TV services.

HISPANIC PERCEPTIONS ON PROTECTIVE RELATIONSHIPS VS. RELATIONSHIPS AMONG EQUALS

	HISPANIC PROTECTIVE VALUES	AMERICAN EQUALITY VALUES
WORK	SEEK BOSS' OR SUPERVISOR'S FRIENDSHIP IN ORDER TO OBTAIN PROTECTION	SEPARATION OF JOB AND PERSONAL LIFE. NO RELIANCE ON BOSS OR FRIEND FOR PROTECTION
FAMILY	PARENTS PROTECT CHILDREN AND ARE PROTECTED BY THEM IN OLD AGE PARENTS HOLD SWAY AT TIMES LIKE CHOOSING A COLLEGE	INDEPENDENCE VALUED, ADULTS FEAR BEING LEFT IN OLD-AGE HOME IN LATER YEARS
SOCIAL LIFE	MAN PROTECTS FIANCÉE HOSTS PROVIDE EVERYTHING FOR A PARTY	EQUALITY BETWEEN MARRIAGE PARTNERS AND FRIENDS
CIVIL AFFAIRS	PATERNALISTIC GOVERNMENTS	CIVIL RIGHTS
BRANDS	NON-CONFRONTATIONAL BRANDS NEED NOT LIVE UP TO EXPECTATIONS LITTLE FEEDBACK SERVICES MORE CONCERNED WITH EXTENDING COVERAGE THAN IN SEEKING TO STAND OUT	BRANDS ASSERTIVELY CONFRONT PAY HEED TO CONSUMERS AND LEARN FROM THEM HUMAN CONTACT SOMETIMES LACKING
	EMOTION-ORIENTED	**RESULTS-ORIENTED**

HISPANIC PERCEPTIONS ON PROTECTIVE RELATIONSHIPS VS. RELATIONSHIPS AMONG EQUALS

	HISPANIC FLEXIBLE SYSTEM	AMERICAN RIGID SYSTEM
WORK	JOB SLACKNESS ALLOWED AS HEALTHY	NO SLACKNESS ON THE JOB
	MORE HOURS ON THE JOB	ADHERENCE TO WORK HOURS
FAMILY	NEGOTIABLE RULES AND CERTAIN LIBERTIES (LIKE CONSUMING ALCOHOL AND TOBACCO)	COMPLIANCE WITH THE NORMS, WHICH ARE ALWAYS OPEN TO QUESTION
SOCIAL LIFE	DROPPING IN UNANNOUNCED IS OK	GET-TOGETHERS ARE PLANNED AND HAVE FIXED TIME-OF-ARRIVAL AND DEPARTURE
	A REAL PARTY IS NOT OVER UNTIL THE LAST GUEST LEAVES	
CIVIL AFFAIRS	SYSTEM ALLOWS FOR "GETTING AROUND" MINOR INFRACTIONS	FIRM LAWS STRONGLY ENFORCED WITH COERCIVE METHODS
BRANDS	ASSUME PRODUCT CONTENT TO BE NEGOTIABLE	TOE THE LINE, DON'T MISLEAD OR TELL HALF-TRUTHS
	SOMETIMES THEY DON'T DELIVER WHAT'S PROMISED	
	SUBJECTIVITY	**LITERALITY**

The second major contrast Hispanics note is how people relate to rules and norms. Just like anywhere else, rules and norms in Latin American countries foster order and progress. However, they are flexibly structured. Hispanics are amazed by the inflexibility of the rules in the U.S. They know that in the homeland they wouldn't have to comply so strictly with such rules.

In their view, the advantage of a society with firmly delineated norms is that it's a stable, functional environment, in which getting what one wants doesn't depend on the ability to circumvent, deal with or slip through the system's cracks. The disadvantage for many is that it makes planning necessary. Not infrequently, the first generations take out loans they're unable to pay back or incur in second mortgages to keep up with the payments. These wellsprings of culture-clash and inter-generational conflicts will be examined further along.

The subject brings up a noteworthy characteristic of Hispanics: ingenuity. Dealing with the vicissitudes of a system in which the laws are flexible requires some creativity, so allowances are made for the improvisations required. In this light, brands that comprehend rule-bending can recur to ironic* communication that humorously celebrates spontaneity and being different.

*(BUT NOT MOCKING!)

In sum, there can be pitfalls for Hispanic-oriented advertising, marketing and market research agencies in focusing too much on cultural differences. Though it might seem less appealing, it's much more effective to concentrate on Hispanic culture's distinctive worthy qualities than on how it differs from American culture.

For example, portrayals of the carefree Hispanic have for years been scoring hits for brands like Corona Beer, because the embellishments on the stereotypical laid-back Latino attitude depict a relaxation ideal to counterbalance a rigid system, which appeals to both Hispanics and the multicultural American society at large.

As we shall see further on, when Hispanics longingly recall cultural aspects of their home countries, often the ideal they picture is in truth undesirable. Their ongoing idealized discourse illuminates many comparison-rooted ambivalent behaviors that should be carefully taken into account.

HIGHLIGHTS

The Hispanic reality is of contrasts, which leads them to appreciate concepts like equality and opportunity inasmuch as they have different meanings in the home culture

Arriving in the U. S. triggers comparing cultures and finding differences between the homeland and the new country

The comparisons continue on into the second generation and to some extent the third

Contrasts often lead them to such painful judgments that they painstakingly avoid forming an opinion about whether certain aspects of the other culture are "better" or "worse"

Researchers can become confused by discourse stemming from culture contrasting, as Hispanics may idealize aspects of a culture that are not necessarily the way they think they are

The main **cultural contrasts** are:

Protection/loyalty vs. **equality**

Flexible system vs. **rigid system**

CHAPTER 3

BEWARE *Ideal-izations*

BASED

on CULTU

CO TR ST

!

By now we're aware that Hispanics modify their views about their homelands after coming to the United States due in large part to the contrasts they observe as they go about their lives. Comparing life in the U.S. with the one they might have had in the old country persists even to some extent into the second and third generations. A romanticized image of certain cultural aspects can easily stem from idealizing their parents' life experiences or from their own trips back home, where they attempt to confirm these accounts with their own eyes.

But the chain of idealizing and romanticizing doesn't end there. As we have seen, it stretches into life in the United States, which is constantly being compared to the "parallel life" they might have had, for better or for worse, in Latin America. It's not that they idealize all aspects of the old country, but rather the defects of one culture are viewed as virtues of the other.

When Hispanics idealize certain aspects, they are seeking to get the best from both cultures. But care must be taken: their discourse can become slanted in the process. Idealization of the American way can lead to not talking about the defects of the United States, while idealization of the Latin American way can cover up the region's real flaws with clichés.

The idealization discourse, as a matter of fact, seeds campaigns or messages aimed at Hispanic communities that place too much emphasis on, for instance, family values or festiveness, without making reference to deeper needs. If we are mindful of the idealized slant in their accounts, though, we understand the true needs of the market in question. This doesn't mean to imply that they are personal or untrue narratives but rather that they serve as "storage" for other needs more difficult to accept and, of course, to explain.

In regard to the idealization of their original cultures, representative themes generally have to do with values of connection and indifference to materiality. At the other extreme, the most appreciated values in the American cultural context are linked with effort and respect for the law. They are two sides of the same coin, and it would seem that were one to win out, the other would lose.

In the bargain, one must consider that the exaggeration of these "opposing sides" is a process that stems from the dynamic of contrasts that Hispanic society experiences and should not necessarily be followed to the letter of the law. And it is certainly true they cannot be totally discarded, but one must understand the needs or the deficiencies hidden behind each idealized attribute.

THE IDEALIZATION OF LATIN AMERICAN VALUES

One of the most persistent clichés in Hispanic discourse is the cohesiveness and compatibility of family life. Some go so far as to find fault in the lack of togetherness and con- geniality among American families when describing the uni- ty they desire in their own family. Beyond the cultural dif- ference between each group's dynamics, this exaggeration and polarization in the discourse about family are directly related to the scarcity of social networks rooted in the very nature of migration.

Feeling alone and unprotected naturally creates nostalgia for the family left behind and the social network it symbolizes. This affects even their children and grandchildren, whose cousins, aunts and uncles are not present in their daily lives. The real search is not for "Latin American-style" family ties but for a network of friends and acquaintances they can count on and with whom they can socialize.

It is true that Hispanics' status as immigrants or children and grandchildren of immigrants motivates them to compensate the loss of connection in their lives by forming community ties. However, it is this selfsame idealized community that sets off a vicious circle that distances them from a more encompassing social life. As a first-generation Hispanic in Chicago put it, "We Hispanics are like crabs: *buddy, buddy*. But if one tries to get ahead, the rest pull him back." This idealization ends up distracting them from the real need hidden beneath the discourse. Just think of the thousands of Hispanics who have not learned English after having lived in the United States for years.

Another Hispanic idealization, the figure of the mother, is pictured as even more nurturing and self-sacrificing. Beyond the ideal, the Latin American devotion to the mother may be masking the wish to acknowledge the role of the homemaker in a country where 60% of women over 17 work[1] and 73% of

[1] BUREAU OF LABOR. COMPARED TO COUNTRIES LIKE MEXICO WHERE ONLY 40% OF ADULT WOMEN WORK.

I miss Colombia all year long.

But when I finally go back on vacation,

after two weeks I can't stand being there.

I'm ready to get back to the peace of my

home in New York.

Hispanic man, age 40,
first generation Colombian, New York City

—Politics here is the same dirty game as in Cub

—Come on, Manny, you're such a blowhard..
How can it be like Cuba if we can't complain
about a thing?

—So OK. What I mean is, you peek behind th
curtain and you find the same scandals
as in any other country.

Hispanic couple, second & third generation,
Cuban descent, Miami

the people think the increase of women in the workforce has been positive.[2]

As in the case of idealization of the family, conformance with the motherhood ideal is not total. Clearly, not all Hispanic women aspire to be homemakers, but as in the example just given, there are times when Hispanic housewives feel undervalued in a society that prizes productivity more than maternity. In idealizing the mother, what they really want to express is the need to recognize Hispanic women's ability to give warmth, affection, stability and care.

Festivity, another idealized value, symbolizes breaking rules, or better yet, having the flexibility to make breaking them acceptable. Let's recall that one of the strongest cultural contrasts that Hispanics experience is having to adapt to complying with strict norms always and forever. Due to this, on those occasions when the job is wearing on them, Hispanics turn nostalgic for the world of flexible rules and the out-of-control *fiesta*... at least in their imagination.

[2] PEW RESEARCH CENTER.

On the other hand, they counter the overriding materiality through acts of generosity or of a religious nature, which are supposedly more common to Latin American societies. They fall back on these discourses when in truth underneath lies a wish to transcend or a desire to mitigate feelings of failure to meet the American consumer culture head-on.

THE IDEALIZATION OF AMERICAN VALUES

Before analyzing the most common idealization discourses in reference to American society, it must be noted that, here, the process is quite different. If they exaggerate its advantages and attributes, it is not due to inadequacies, as in the Latin American case, but is rather a result of comparison. For example, it's common for Hispanics to criticize the U.S. political system, yet they don't view it as worse than the one back home because they usually believe it's less corrupt. In reality, they're voicing their disappointment at encountering faults in a system they had pictured as totally upright.

Other idealized features of the United States include lawfulness and efficient law enforcement, discipline, patriotism and world leadership. Exaggerated idealization can lead them to gloss over their exasperation at feeling adrift amidst the rigidity, the homesickness, the discrimination and corruption.

Ultimately, it could prove counterproductive for them to exaggerate either country's cultural traits, as it could lead them unawares into the realm of stereotyping. Hence, they try to balance the necessities of getting along without forgetting, or exaggerating the home culture's values.

For second-generation Hispanics, the process might be the reverse. In attempting to deal with cultural values, they exaggerate (at least in their parents' eyes) the advantages of the American ones. It's not uncommon for them to turn into law-abiding American patriots and join, for instance, the Border Patrol or the army: attitudes their parents often don't understand.

The reason, as we saw in the last chapter, is found within the multicultural context. Once they've perceived they are a part of a cultural mosaic, they moderate the idealizing based on contrasting the two cultures. This process takes place at all income levels, as it is unlikely that Hispanics would come in contact with just two cultural realities, much less one. Their relationship with the U.S. encompasses more cultures than their own.

Awareness of the fact that America is a multicultural construct helps them on their way to finding their own place and voice in the social dynamic. Contrarily, if they only perceive two cultures, they have the impression these are opposed. This has nothing to do with the usual multicultural discourse but rather with communicating from a different distance. Becoming aware of all the cultures makes it obvious that Americans and Hispanics have much in common. It would be advantageous to know how to use them as multicultural interpreters.

HIGHLIGHTS

At times, culture contrasting leads Hispanics to idealize their home culture while magnifying American traits

Idealization of Latin American values can be a cover-up of real needs such as having an extended circle of friends they can count on similar to what they would have back home, particularly among the first generation

Idealized American values can be a cover for feeling out of step with the local culture or small social or political disappointments that don't meet their extremely high expectations of the U.S.

This is particularly so among the second generation, which aggrandizes American values, especially around their parents

Both processes
are like microscopes
that reveal root causes
but not their
true dimensions

Hence, the best way
to avoid distortions of
the idealizing discourse is by
way of a multicultural point of
view that gives context and
dimension to the two cultures,
which are not opposites;
they're complementary

Chapter 4

dlR
de la Riva group

The

HISPANIC

GAME

As we have seen, three basic conditioners determine the behavior of Hispanics in the United States:

- A stereotyping label they wish to shed.
- The need to validate themselves and prove their worth to both the United States and the home (or forebears') country.
- Constant access to two cultural referents, the U. S. and the homeland.

In light of this situation, Hispanics face a very complex process on their way to building an identity. The main dilemma is to find the best formula that would allow them to get on with life in the United States and make themselves an asset. Some do it better than others, but everyone ends up asking themselves the same questions. To what degree am I Hispanic or American? In which contexts? Which is less stereotyping?

Let's assume that the first three generations of Hispanics unquestioningly accept that part of their identity is determined by their heritage and by their "Latino" features. At the same time, another part depends on the American codes and values they have taken on. In this way, Hispanics have no other option than to get along and play with both influences because they have two lenses with which to view the same reality.

All Hispanics, even those well assimilated into American society, face the predicament of feeling obligated to use both cultural referents, as both codes are in play at the same time. As we'll see in Chapter 5, this clash is not resolved by a Hispanic assimilating and becoming completely American but rather by learning to manage his cultural influences and assign preferences for them or even rise above them.

To this day, the way Hispanics resolve the quandary is through strategically deploying their cultural resources. That is to say, they choose according to the context of the moment, which facet to feature, American or Hispanic, in order to validate themselves.

One of the most common manifestations of this can be clearly noted in language usage. As a second-generation bilingual Hispanic stated, the English he uses with his American coworkers is unaccented and well pronounced because it behooves him to not play on his Latino background. But when he's with other Hispanics, he Latinizes his accent and mixes in some Spanish to show that he is linked with his heritage and at ease with it. He feels perfectly validated on both accounts.

Consumption also brings this behavior into play. As we have said, brands, products and services—essential for communicating who they are—have a starring role in Hispanic identity building. Consequently, if we open a typical Hispanic family refrigerator, we wouldn't be surprised to find a mix of American and Latino drinks. Quite likely there would be American soft drinks alongside fresh-fruit flavored *aguas frescas*. It would be interesting to find out how they arrived at their choices of drinks. What do they want each to communicate?

We liken the strategy of featuring Hispanic or American attributes to a Lego game. At their disposal are pink pieces (Hispanic) and blue ones (American), and they use both colors to build their identity. They incorporate elements from both cultures to form a heterogeneous identity that combines multiple codes which enable them to express themselves to their best advantage. Hence, they have not passed through the melting pot. That would be too limiting. More than becoming a cultural blend, Hispanics possess strategic identity.

Accordingly, when applying for admission to a college, they might stress the fact they're Hispanic to take advantage of the ethnic quota system. Once they're in, though, they behave on campus like typical American college students. They might even choose to study out of state, a break with the Hispanic custom of offspring living at home for as long as possible.

But this strategic behavior does not prevent organizing the Hispanic market in differentiated segments. As we shall see further along, deciding which pieces to choose is directly related to how open they are to the host culture's codes and those of their heritage. Consequently, some Hispanics are more receptive and willing to adopt American ways, and others prefer to carry on with traditions. In either case, we will always find contexts in which the strategic game is at play.

This means that to really understand Hispanics we should be mindful of this bi-dimensioned cultural ability, as the decision to buy our product or contract our services is a function of it. We need to pause and figure out if what we're selling can be cataloged among the choices Hispanics make according to Latino codes or American ones. When buying insurance, do they rely on their Latino legacy of not minding unsure footing or their American side that seeks control over the surroundings?

Our main task when approaching this market is to understand which pieces the Hispanic will play with when comparing our product, pink ones or blue ones? What does he want to emphasize at that moment. To whom does he wish to prove his worth? Returning to the drinks, it's quite likely he'll choose a soft drink that shows him belonging to the crowd that consumes one of the country's emblematic products. It's a simple statement, "Check me out, I'm just like you. We drink the same soda pop." From this, it logically follows that he is less likely to consume soft drinks from the old country, as that does not communicate to the public the identity he wishes to project. Regardless of how tradition-bound a Hispanic might be, in this instance he plays his blue pieces.

The same thing happens when we consider other categories. Do they buy beer according to American or Hispanic criteria? Which side do they want to project? In what contexts? Perhaps a first-generation Hispanic, a noted nostalgia-prone group, might decide for American criteria and buy Bud Light. On the other hand, a third-generation Hispanic, whom we are tempted to characterize as very Americanized, might prefer Corona beer or Mezcal Delirio to emphasize his Latino roots and authenticate himself in certain situations.

Obviously, beyond their heritage, Hispanics are human beings who seek out what serves them best. It shouldn't come as a surprise that they make consumer decisions on neither American nor Latino leanings but simply having to do with price or convenience. Such would be the case of generic brands where, in the absence of appreciable cultural connotations, there is more neutrality. Or indeed any other category whose motives for buying are not linked to identity.

In this sense it is important for brands, products and services to have a clear idea as to the extent their category comes into play in the identity-game strategy. Probably a spaghetti sauce or dishwashing detergent need not pay any mind to this scenario and simply focus on competing with traditional-style marketing strategies. Attempting to enter the game by embellishing no-name brands with cultural elements would be cumbersome and forced.

From this perspective, as brand managers we should ask ourselves if our brand or category plays a part in this strategic use of identities and thereafter assess it by means of the proper market research methodologies and techniques.

If indeed the brand, category or product falls within the playing field of strategic identity, then the tactics to achieve successful communication should stem from careful analysis. In order to facilitate this, here's a short checklist to help in thinking out a brand's function and objectives in this scenario:

QUESTION	TACTIC
DOES MY BRAND REITERATE STEREOTYPES? WHICH STEREOTYPES?	IDENTIFY STEREOTYPING AND GET RID OF IT AS MUCH AS POSSIBLE
DOES MY BRAND AID IN VALIDATION? IS IT VALIDATION IN THE U.S.A. OR ESSENTIALLY AMONG HISPANICS?	IDENTIFY AVENUES FOR VALIDATION TO TAKE PLACE, AS WELL AS ITS MEANING.
IS THE DECISION FOR MY BRAND BASED ON AMERICAN OR HISPANIC CRITERIA?	RECOGNIZE WHICH CRITERIA HOLDS SWAY IN THE DECISION TO BUY

In the context of everything we have seen, the strategic identity game comes naturally to Hispanics. People, no matter our origins, play with identity according to the image we wish to project to others, and technology has become a major ally. If we think about the image people construct for themselves on social networks like Twitter, we find out that it's not necessarily distinct from the real person. They do, however, spotlight certain preferred or positive aspects such as intelligence, sense of humor, sensitivity and so on. Everyone strategically chooses which portrait to show according to the circumstances.

Hence, it ought not come as a surprise how Hispanics play with their cultural referents. What could be more natural? What is to be noted is that this custom affects their choices of purchase and thus the rules that will prevail in the United States Hispanic market in the coming years. What interests us is which themes of influence will be left standing and prevailing. Every category must take it upon itself to know and measure over time which cultural trait dictates the rules, under what conditions and how Hispanics are playing their pieces.

Hispanics strategically use their Latino and American referents to build their identity

Their identity is not a **blend** but rather a **combination** of elements

They stress their American or Hispanic features according to which best validates them

Their buying and consuming decisions are influenced by the identity they wish to reinforce at that moment

Chapter 5

The

GENERATIONS

dlR
de la Riva group

Identity isn't acquired merely by arriving at a major decision shaped through time and cultural contact. It has, rather, to do with many small but highly strategic choices made day in and day out. Simple decisions when Hispanics trot out or hide their heritage culture or the American culture they've acquired depend mostly on what suits them at the time.

These small choices are made on the job, out shopping and, most importantly, at home, where their ongoing selection of Lego pieces affects the family dynamic and is a source of parent-offspring discord.

Hispanics are usually segmented by generation, in which case we find such a wide variance that we often forget they're part of the same family and eat supper together every evening. They are a part of the same system and each has a role.

Accordingly, all members of a Hispanic family play distinct roles that no one else can assume, which impacts on identity building. In addition, assumption of a role influences the way other members do what corresponds to them.

The parents, the first generation, are transmitters of Hispanic ways par excellence. They are the family chroniclers in charge of keeping others aware of what it means to be from the old country. To do so, they create a mythic image of the homeland and, in addition, a concept of how the rest of the family members should carry on the heritage. Despite this symbol-laden narrative being so fundamental to the evolution of the Hispanic family in the United States, parents are often unconscious of the fact and are unable to assess how important their stories are to their children and grandchildren. Throughout this chapter we shall see why the manner in which the stories are told is crucial to the second and third generations' identity.

Parents naturally tend to revert to their Latin American condition when choosing their Lego pieces, as the majority of their referents are from the original culture. This doesn't mean they play their American pieces less strategically than other family members. In fact, in the extensive anthropological fieldwork we did for our study, it wasn't unusual to "happen upon" American brands hidden in the cupboards (often beer, as we've noted), which they show off to local friends at significant moments, even if they swear eternal allegiance to the homeland.

The second generation, their offspring, play the difficult to fulfill role of cultural interpreters, as expectations for these "Americans" of the family are frequently outlandish. Nevertheless, the parents unwittingly consider them "pseudo-Americans" and can easily introduce them as, "This is Junior; he thinks he's American." As the children grow, there's a tacit agreement that they take charge of explaining to parents or visiting acquaintances what it means "to be American". Second-generation Hispanics are also in charge of telling parents whenever the latter unwittingly break American cultural codes, for instance, a parent's embarrassing habit of shouting into his cell-phone in public: unmannerly in the U.S.A.

Offspring tend to deploy more blue Lego pieces, even though deciding on an identity to adopt for daily living is usually a tough job, much of it due to the first generation's customary hopes that the kids will be "the Americans" of the family. Still, as parents, they feel underappreciated if the kids become "too" American and even more so if they reject some Latin American customs. The second generation's struggle for validation tends to be more intense, because they understand the mechanisms that can dump them into stereotype.

What's more, even though they still love and respect their parents, they feel out of touch with the old country.

Finally, the grandchildren take on the role of redeemers or re-inventors of what it means to be Hispanic. In principle, their identity and cultural belonging are not under question as the second generation was. Additionally, they usually come along when the culture clash has subsided a bit. The third generation generally arrives when its parents have already gone through adolescence and their search for identity. Now, as Americans, grandchildren have gained a more constructive view of their heritage, which opens up avenues to assign new meanings to their grandparents' cultural background so that it complements American values.

Although marketing studies and advertising don't generally pay much attention to the third generation, our study suggests it is precisely the most creative, culture-wise. These are the people that indicate avenues of approach for brands to follow, because they consume more products from the old country*. They're critical without being overly so and they assist their parents and grandparents in finding their place in American society.

* AS LONG, THAT IS, AS THEY ARE IN HARMONY WITH THEIR AMERICAN ENVIRONS.

upper's ready, cheese sandwiches.

Ve mostly all eat together, so please forgive

'ony, who always eats supper alone in his room.

Ie's our most American member.

Hispanic woman, age 35, second generation,
Mexican descent, Austin

If you asked me about Hispanic people which I really admire, my answer would be: My Parents. But I think that we still need a contemporary Hispanic figure, someone who makes us feel proud, but not a celebrity or a singer; they sometimes make me feel embarrassed. Maybe a leader or a politician who could inspire us, and make us feel proud as a group... And who knows, maybe one day we could even have a Hispanic president, just how it happened with Obama and the African-American community, it could happen to us... I really hope so!!!

Hispanic woman, age 18, second generation,
Mexican descent, Los Angeles

The grandchildren tend to adhere to an American identity that they only abandon if it's to their extreme advantage to do so. Their American identity, however, includes an awareness of the family heritage, along with a certain pride, not unlike so many other descendants of immigrants.

THE SACRIFICE THAT PRODUCES CULTURAL CLASHES, NOT ENCOUNTERS

As we mentioned, many second and third-generation identity conflicts stem from the parents' or grandparents' stories about coming to the United States. These accounts naturally differ from family to family, but their central theme is sacrifice. Parents or grandparents relate the sacrifice they made in leaving the homeland to achieve a goal, whatever it might be.

The tales of their beginnings in turn seed the following generations' attitudes and undertakings. Although they are apt to take the story somewhat for granted, the children will hear it, interspersed with quips about the differences between the homeland and the new one, over and over throughout their lives.

Sacrifice is the means by which a person exchanges a lifestyle, an ideal or even his being in order to transform his world. This spirit permeates Hispanic family relations. The manner in which the parents' sacrifice is told, becoming modified with children and grandchildren, is a great narrative opportunity for brands that understand it, because it is a doorway into the private lives of Hispanics and presents a puzzle to be solved.

The story of a sacrifice that paid off significantly inclines families to be much more open to American culture. Contrarily, a sacrifice that didn't deliver what parents had hoped for their children and grandchildren is apt to be a root cause of family conflict, as well as major difficulties in adapting to American ways.

Moving to another country implies sacrificing something for a greater good. If after a time immigrants aren't doing as well as they'd hoped and haven't obtained what they sacrificed for, the stories they tell differ considerably from the ones told by those who did fulfill their aspirations. For families whose decision to migrate didn't give them a noticeably better quality of life, the story usually portrays the original immigrant as the victim who sacrificed himself for the good of his children. These parents are likely to experience the sacrifice from a personal perspective, assuming the role of martyr and displaying a self-denying attitude among people who idealize the heritage culture. It's not unusual for them to constantly state their intention to return to the old country some day, even though they're not seriously planning to do so anytime soon.

The offspring therefore come under a lot of pressure to "benefit" from and show their "gratitude" for their parent's sacrifice, while also being expected to successfully acquire an American identity. But they are expected to have respect for their heritage culture and are severely recriminated should they find fault with it: a likely source of much conflict. This, alongside the expectations to become American, often puts the children in the position of feeling obliged to defend their identity against intrusions of family behavior by forcing a "Super-American" front.

Grandchildren, for their part, are apt to become the conciliators between generations. Insofar as they establish some distance, they are able to contextualize the family's story and distill what is of worth.

Let's now examine the opposite case. Some families feel the decision to emigrate has paid off with a better quality of life. Generally these came in legally or found what they esteem a much better job. Here, the first generation does not think of itself as a sacrificial martyr but rather as the heroic figure in the family's founding myth. Here, attitudes are notably open and flexible in regard to American culture and the American ways their children have assimilated.

In all cases, the grandchildren, buffered by generational distance, are afforded a more objective view of the sacrifice as something to always remember as a tribute to the family patriarch. The grandparents' self-sacrifice doesn't usually burden the grandchildren, unless the conflicts have been passed along to them.

Obviously, the story of the sacrifice is quite significant in Hispanic family life, not just because of the outcome but because it is the foundation upon which the family builds its sense of validation and authenticity.

THE FIRST GENERATION'S STORY:
THE PARENTS' ARRIVAL IN THE UNITED STATES

It could be said the parents came to the United States as explorers, in that they generally weren't sure of what they would find and simply desired a better life. The motive to migrate differs between men and women and, accordingly, they have different discourses.

Men are apt to say they left the homeland in their role as providers. Work dominates their discourse. But the woman's story has more to do with being a wife and mother. Hers is a discourse of love.

Furthermore, her coming is also conditioned by the intention to return to the home country, regardless of whether she ever actually does so.

If a woman is of a mind to return, she continuously assesses herself to make sure she's behaving in accord with the home culture, making it harder to open up to the American way and expecting the children to do it for her. The women have a different view of American culture, noting that at the personal level, it creates lots of jobs, yet it's threatening, lacking in values and discriminatory. They often realize that the occasional discrimination they experience is not so much due to their origins but to their behavior anchored in the old country's codes.

They tend to work a lot, save whatever they can and spend less. They cut expenses by living in cramped quarters and buying the bare necessities. It's common for their houses to be bereft of décor as though they might leave at any minute, even if they've lived in the same place for years. They can stay isolated in their barrios and never venture out to see the sights.

On the other hand, the ones who have in mind settling down long range have the opposite attitude. They are apt to open up to American culture and give their children open passage to both cultures. If they feel discriminated against, they take stock of the situation to figure out if it was caused by the way they were acting or because of their origin. They view American culture as a source of long-range individual and family opportunities. They seek to integrate themselves and their children, and if they move, they try to avoid changing

They aren't Mexicans now. They don't know what it is to slave away for a pittance.

Hispanic woman, age 45,
first generation Mexican, Chicago

When I was a kid in Guatemala, the United Fruit Company built a club and swimming pool that the Guatemalan kids couldn't enter. I think about that sometimes. Here I had to wait three years to become president of the Ear, Nose and Throat Association, when other Americans became president in a year. His wife asks, 'Are you sure it's because of that? Wasn't the club just for the workers' kids?' 'Maybe,' he replies, 'but all of them were Americans. So what do you say about how long it took for me to be president?'

Hispanic couple, first generation Guatemalan, Miami

schools, even when they are in another district. Overall, they respect and value American law and order and the long-term advantages of the United States.

On the job, they seek to acquire skills that help them advance and prosper. They consume products that enable them to express their personality, such as decorative items for the home. They explore American culture with *gusto* and try to become acquainted with their city.

AN UNEXPECTED COMFORT ZONE

To be sure, there are differences in the way the immigration stories affect the progress of Hispanic families. Naturally, there are also similarities among first-generation Hispanics. No matter whether they plan to stay or go back, all immigrants are amazed to find attributes that bestow a sense of security. Finding a familiar milieu such as entire Spanish-speaking communities and products they're accustomed to using puts them in a comfort zone.

This familiarity contrasts with the discovery of things American. They are thrilled to explore a totally new culture that reveals features of their own that they had been unaware of. Brands take part in the Hispanic game of feeling on familiar footing and the excitement of exploring the new American milieu.

THE WASTE EFFECT

Once the initial excitement has subsided and they've established the discourse they employ to justify their being in the United States, they start to feel comfortable with American brands. Thus they take up the custom of passing along used, but still serviceable, shoes or not eating everything on their plate. Once they've gotten used to spending in dollars without having to calculate in the homeland currency, they start buying more brand-name products, especially people from less privileged backgrounds who had been unable to do so before.

This is significant both for the Hispanic market in the United States and the Latin American communities it hails from, as the latter get relevant information about brand names in addition to regularly receiving care packages of semi-new shoes and apparel, as we've pointed out.

After a spell of this waste effect, first-generation Hispanics feel a bit empty and blame it on the way they spend their money. They figure they wouldn't have done such a thing back in the old country. At the same time, they realize that although the name brands are reasonably priced and they can afford them, services are much more expensive than back home.

Practically all of them take notice that the jump in quality of living was at the level of consumer products, and they grow weary. They go through a phase in which they tire of excessive buying and prestigious brands. Eventually they reflect on the cultural nuances of brands and services, all the while gaining an appreciation for significant factors in their life such as the secure American society and their children's stability. Even so, it's a nostalgic, although temporary process, during which they tend to return to homeland brands. First-generation Hispanics who have resided for some time in the United States perceive discourses rooted in the nostalgia driver as tiresome and worn out. They would rather move forward!

Sonia:

"Love made me cross the border"

Sonia, who doesn't use make up, is 28. She's humorous and slow-moving. When she tells us her story, our first impression is that it's fictional, like a soap opera.

Sonia was on the verge of finishing her nursing studies when her boyfriend Jorge proposed marriage. Jorge had illegally crossed the border several times and wanted to take her back to the United States and settle down. Sonia rightly rues that she just lacked one semester to get her degree, which would have come in handy in New York; but instead of negotiating the move's timing and conditions with Jorge, she didn't stand up for herself and went along with him.

"I didn't know where we were going, I just wanted to be at his side, so you might say it was love that brought me to the United States. On the way, some things happened that made me wonder if I'd done the right thing, but there was no going back and I didn't want to be without Jorge; I was so in love. We crossed a desert in a truck, me sitting up front between two cocaine-snorting smugglers. I just kept my mouth shut and prayed. I kept wondering, 'What are these guys going to do to me? Are we going to crash?' Jorge was stashed away in back with some others and couldn't see or do anything."

Sonia is no longer an innocent, though, having by now twice gone through the process of going back to her hometown in Michoacán, becoming bored and returning to the United States. The second time around, she went to New York.

"The worst is when you finally get here and the smugglers shut you into a room with other families. We were about 15 people living in the room, waiting for our families to pay for the crossing. They weren't going to let us out until they got their money, and we were scared because we didn't know if our families could pay or what would happen to us if they upped the price or didn't get their money. We'd look out the window to see the city, but all we saw was more apartments. The worst, though, was not knowing what the smugglers that had got us across might do. They were always threatening us."

After three weeks of absolutely no privacy, Sonia and her husband got out of the waiting room and he quickly got a job cooking at an Irish restaurant in the Bronx. "All the Irish restaurants hire Mexicans to cook because of our work ethic. We're not like Puerto Ricans. They live on unemployment."

They took a small flat two blocks away. Shortly thereafter, Sonia got pregnant and had a son they named Junior. His parents consider him American because he was born in New York and has some rights. But they've not registered his birth for fear of being deported, and they don't take him to the doctor when he gets sick.

Even so, amidst all the family's gray areas,
they need a government service because of
(no surprise) Junior's English. Neither Sonia
nor Jorge speak it and have never needed
it. Nevertheless, Sonia detected a language
problem in Junior that requires a state
therapist's house call three times a week.
When Sonia introduces her three year-old son,
she says, "This is Junior, sorry, he doesn't
understand Spanish… He thinks he's American."

We were with them for some time and thus were
able to figure out that there's no need for
Junior to talk. Before he can do anything,
Sonia does it for him. His speech impediment
keeps him out of kindergarten, so she denies
her needs in order to attend to his. Hence,
she can't work. "I could have been a nurse,
and here they're paid well. But, you know, you
can never do enough for your kids."

Consumption in Sonia's family demonstrates
the game of Mexican and American role playing
in the home. The apartment is spotless but

sparsely decorated, giving the impression they're ready to pack up and go back to Michoacán. Their biggest outlays are on electronics and toys for Junior, who's in control of the iPad and all the rest, as though it were his right as an American.

Other expenditures are for the family. Sonia doesn't buy cosmetics or fashions. Her game is coupons and comparing prices. The one luxury they allow for is gifts for Mexico, from pirated movies to Chinese costume jewelry. They shop the neighborhood stores (Hispanic, Asian and American) hunting for items that catch the eye. They guilelessly asked the anthropologists if they thought this or that item could be found in Mexico.

"I can't figure out what to send to my cousins. Sometimes Jorge feels bad about trashing his old sneakers, so he sends them. We send everything because, you know, in Mexico, they need it."

When the anthropologists ask them if they've
shopped for gifts in Manhattan, Sonia finds
a space between the apartments lining
the street where she can see the tips of
skyscrapers on the island and blatantly
admits, "We've not gone that far. One time I
went walking and got to the church, but I'm
not familiar with those parts so I came back."

INVERTED NOSTALGIA

However, there is a nostalgia at play that goes unnoticed, despite being even more advantageous for brands: inverted nostalgia. Let's recall that Hispanics tend to become opinion leaders in their hometowns, and a major facet of this role is informing their families about brands and products.

Creatives, publicists, communicators and media buyers should pay close attention to this. Hispanics are bombarded day after day with so many messages trying to hook into their cultural identity that they become oversaturated and start blocking out any event, product or service of this ilk, whereupon they settle into just trying to be regular Americans. On another front, there are increasingly fewer American products that can't be obtained in Latin America, especially in Mexico. These two factors in their lives can diminish their role as opinion leaders and senders or receivers of brands. They develop an inverse nostalgia for borders that no longer exist and start seeking out hard-to-find products in the U.S. to send to the folks back home or home-country products they themselves can consume in order to enhance their American side.

For American brands, the flow of products and trends into Latin American communities is a major opportunity that's largely underexploited. But the ones already taking advantage of it are pretty happy for happening upon it. Let's also recall that in their desire to feel part of the global community of trendsetters, Hispanics are thankful to live in the United States and enjoy easy access to name brands. In addition to seeking out brands that make them trend leaders in their communities, they want to feel symbolically reinforced by them. In other words, even if they don't send name brands to the hometown, it's nice to live in the midst of outstanding American products. Consequently, special editions and seasonal versions are so significant, as they symbolize the remarkable options they've "discovered" in the United States; a real treasure for this segment of explorers.

As we've stated, all the stories about the first generation's experiences get told time and again, to be soaked up by their children. The parents' stories never die, because their children are constantly hearing them. In the doing, the latter don't just get a story, they are handed a role to fulfill.

Arturo:

"Neither culture is better than the other"

Arturo, a successful surgeon, was born in Guatemala. His wife, also a Guatemalan, is an especially gracious hostess. Their home in Miami gives the feeling it was designed with socializing in mind. Our conversation takes off in their impressive kitchen with a platter of cupcakes and a view of the backyard and pool. Their two sons are married to Americans.

His immigration history begins well before coming to the United States, as his work as an ophthalmologist had taken him all over Latin America. On the strength of his curriculum vita, he got a job offer from a hospital in Miami, which he initially was inclined to turn down. The whole house is tastefully decorated with contemporary objects, except the books and an antique sewing machine that occupies a privileged spot in the home. Obviously it's there as a springboard for Arturo to launch into his favorite stories.

"I did my social service in Quiriguá, a village in Guatemala. The town was so needy I was thinking to stay right there, as the doctors were kilometers away and I made myself useful. One time I made a house call on a villager's mother who was very ill. I knew he was really poor, but I thought, 'So he can't pay me… No big deal.' When I got through attending to her I gave them some medicine and told him not to worry about his mother's health. As I was about to leave, he paid me with the only thing of value that belonged to him, this sewing machine. I was so moved that I took it. Besides, it would have been a grave offense if I hadn't. Years later I got it restored because it has a lot of meaning for me.

Although his sons are thinking of moving out of state, Arturo wouldn't want to live anywhere else but Miami. "Miami is really special for people who've come from Latin America. No other town in the country welcomes you like Miami." His American daughter-in-law immediately backs him up, allowing as how Hispanics truly

feel at home in Miami and that even one of
her own sisters moved to Nebraska because she
didn't like for so many Hispanics to be flowing
in. Sensing she might have said something
offensive to her in-laws, she adds, "She thinks
different than me, though." Her husband, in his
role of all-American guy, doesn't feel alluded
to in any way.

After mulling the question over, Arturo concludes
that the most worthy feature of Guatemalan
culture is the connection with the family. "We
get together just like this every week. Sundays,
we watch the soccer matches together.

On the second day we were with the family,
Arturo invited us to supper with some Hispanic
friends to talk about how they feel about
living in Miami. He reckons the Latino crowd
makes it easier for him to tell stories about
his youth than if he were among Americans.

"All the old guys you see here were once young
guys. And when we were students we were too

poor to eat anywhere else but home. Remember
Sanborn's (a Mexican chain restaurant) gives
you the check at the table and you pay at the
cash register. One of us would go alone to
Sanborn's, sit down and drink a coffee. About
a half hour later, he'd ask for the check and,
when the waitress went to get it, we'd all
come in pretending it was sheer happenstance,
'Hey, Arturo, fancy seeing you here, man!' And
everybody would sit down. We'd order whatever
we wanted, hamburger, enchiladas, mole... We'd
get the second check, but we'd only pay the
first one at the cash register..."

One of his sons happening by breaks in,
flabbergasted, "You did what? Please Dad, you
didn't. What are you guys laughing about?
That's embarrassing; you couldn't afford a
single meal? I bet you damn could." Arturo
motions him to move on and looks at the
Mexican anthropologist, "See what I tell you?
They don't understand anything. I'm sure you
do. Just look at them, they don't have fun
like we used to. We'd be laughing all day."

SECOND GENERATION: THE CHILDREN'S NARRATIVE

For better or for worse, children begin life as an anchor in the United States for their parents, affording stability but impeding movement. Their birth is one more reason to stay in the U.S., and children listen to the parents' immigrant story, especially if both are first generation.

According to the quantitative findings of our study, the Hispanics most admired by the second generation are generally their relatives.

Offspring growing up listening to their parents' tale are partially robbed of center stage, where the parents hold forth as the heroes while they are relegated to the roles of beneficiaries of their sacrifice. It's a heavy load indeed for the children if they are cast solely as beneficiaries and the parents refuse to admit that they, too, enjoy living in the U.S.A.

It is not unusual for parents' to have too many expectations, and as though that weren't enough, their expectations are often contradictory. On the one hand, children are taught to acknowledge and be proud of their heritage and to conserve Hispanic values. But on the other, they are expected to adapt to American culture and get ahead, become a part of the society, take on its values and, without implying a value judgment, recognize that life is better in the United States. In the end, children growing up under such conflicting expectations have a hard time finding a balance.

They also encounter difficulties in defining a cultural stance, and once they do, sticking with it becomes another issue. They feel odd in social situations, but at the same time they don't feel they resemble their parents. It's not surprising then that they tend to socialize with and marry Hispanics of their generation.

They constantly feel under pressure. What's more, defending their American identity turns into a struggle between finding their place in society and not letting the family down. It's no wonder the second generation tends to switch cultural stances more than the others.

They describe their generation's identity as undefined, because they lack a story or myth that endorses them as individuals and as worthy Americans. Notably lacking are role models to inspire and guide them; in fact, they feel that many Hispanic opinion leaders are farfetched figures who might drag them into stereotype. They are in need of a story of their own!

When they grow up and become parents, they try to free their children from the discourse of sacrifice that they heard so many times. They try to raise them to be "normal" Americans who totally pertain to the surrounding culture. At times, they try so hard to set them free that they produce new conflicts in the third generation, but most of the time the latter move beyond the cultural identity problem.

THE GRANDCHILDREN'S STORY: THE THIRD GENERATION

The third generation tends to want to put the conflicts between the parents and grandparents to rest. From their point of view, the heritage culture is more likely to build rather than destroy the Hispanic personality, because rather than completely defining them as Hispanos, it affords them a measure of distinction among other Americans. Thus, some of them turn to re-inventing what it means to be Hispanic. They rediscover elements of their heritage, viewing them afresh without the conflicts they generated among the older generations. Consequently, they are able to reassign meanings to Hispanic elements in such a way that these gain significance alongside American values.

The values the grandchildren rescue become authentically Hispanic, meaning, they've transcended what Americans think of as "Latin American". Let's take a look at a chain of restaurants specializing in Mexican-style *burritos*. The *carnitas*, the *frijoles* and, for sure, the chipotle chiles all taste pretty authentic. But that's not even the beginning of the story. What's fascinating about the chain is its positioning. Sure, it sells burritos and, yes, we know it's a Mexican grill, but the positioning has to do with its gourmet way of making burritos, sourcing sustainably grown, fresh local ingredients and natural, hormone-free meats to prepare "food with integrity". You can order your grilled tacos soft or crispy and read its Webpage in English or Spanish.

In addition to food, the third generation has salvaged femininity, another treasured element. First-generation mothers take it upon themselves to pass along to their daughters tips on perfumes, cosmetics, fashion and dancing. Girls know that Hispanic womanhood's close attention to personal appearance is a mark of distinction and they take to it, transforming details that might have made their grandmothers seem strangely out of place into highly fashionable elements for the younger generations. They play with the classic Hispanic physical characteristics and know how to turn brunette hair, bronze skin, etc. to their advantage.

"My name is Rita, and I don't speak Spanish"

What's most unusual about Rita is she raises
snakes and sells them over the Internet for
a hobby. She inherited the predilection from
her father, a policeman and second-generation
Cuban American living in Miami. We quickly
realize that the fear the snakes evoke is no
minor part of her fascination for the hobby.

Rita is eight years old. She's sociable but
is uncomfortable speaking to us about her
Hispanic roots. "I just don't know. I imagine
Cuba to be a little, I don't know, dusty? Yeah,
dusty, right Mom?" She'd definitely like to
go to Cuba to find out about it. She fetches
from her closet a pair of low-heel shoes her
grandmother gave her. "I love these shoes.
I could just look at them and play with them
forever." But Rita has never worn them, and
they're brand new. "Well, these are dancing
shoes, and I don't know how to dance. But they

are so great. When I learn to walk on heels,
I'll use them."

After talking about the upcoming theme-party
for her birthday, she goes on to tell us about
her school over supper. She ought to have had
to change schools when the family moved to
another district, but she didn't because her
mom wanted her to keep her friends. Afterwards
she shows us the artwork she did this week,
an apple with her photo and a text: "Hello,
my name is Rita. I love apples and snakes. I
have a pet snake named Bill and I don't speak
Spanish."

The identity game is experienced especially in the home where each generation carries out its cultural mission: a source of culture conflict

The degree to which the first generation opens up to American culture and the second to Latin American ways depends on the discourse of sacrifice

If the parents' story implies they came to the United States as a sacrifice for their children, the latter are apt to feel it as a heavy burden and close off to the heritage culture

In all instances,
the third generation has
the potential to reconfigure
Hispanic elements so that
they make sense in the
American context

CHAPTER 6

Identity

Stances

dlR
de la Riva group

By now we've seen that Hispanics play with American and Latino cultural referents in order to construct their identity and validation. Additionally, they choose which facet to feature that will best serve them at a given time. This, in turn, is strongly conditioned by their generational role and how it plays out in the family.

If we were to leave off the analysis at this point, we would be reducing Hispanic identity construction to a mere matter of convenience. This would be quite inadequate, however. Hispanics feel motivated to define their cultural-preference stance, because ambiguity (to be Hispanic, yet not Hispanic) would be of little use in a society that constantly questions where one stands.

And although they make use of their cultural resources as circumstances demand, they truly do demonstrate a preference for and identification with one of their two cultural scenarios. Like everybody, they need an identity that makes them stand out from all others in such a way that in their relations with society at large, other people can identify them as Hispanics or Americans, and they can carry on accordingly. Regardless of factors such as the generation they belong to, the town they live in or their age, this stance is ultimately of their own choosing.

Hence, two main variables are operant when Hispanics decide upon an identity:

● Identification with a nationality, the one with which they feel the most affinity. In other words, to define themselves mainly as "American" or "Hispanic", regardless of birthplace.

● For example, a person raised and educated in Guatemala is more likely to consider himself Hispanic than one who did so in the United States. However, as shown below, some American-born people also think of themselves as Hispanic rather than American. An Argentine (or an American just as well), regardless of birthplace, can identify himself as Hispanic.

			WHERE WERE YOU BORN?	
			IN THE U.S.A.	ELSEWHERE
		TOTAL	A	B
	BASE	1501	670	831
I IDENTIFY MYSELF AS:	HISPANIC / LATINO ONLY	32	9	51A
	EQUALLY HISPANIC / LATINO AMERICAN	26	38B	16
	HISPANIC / LATINO FIRST, AMERICAN SECOND	25	21	28A
	AMERICAN FIRST, HISPANIC SECOND	12	23B	4
	AMERICAN ONLY	4	8B	1
	DON'T KNOW	1	1	1

Significant positive differences at 95% highlighted in green

● Openness in relation to acceptance of the opposite culture from the one chosen as the defining one. In other words, whether they are open or closed to the other culture.

● For example, a person can define himself as Hispanic and be closed to American ways or as a Hispanic who accepts them. The same holds for those who identify themselves as Americans; they can be open or closed to Hispanic ways. Everything depends on the personal decision they've come to regarding how much of the other culture to allow into their lives.

Along these lines, we initially identified four stances that reveal themselves in relation to affinity for a concrete nationality (Hispanic or American) and the degree of cultural openness (open or closed).

IDENTIFICATION WITH A NATIONALITY	ATTITUDE
HISPANIC	● HISPANIC CLOSED TO AMERICAN WAYS
	● HISPANIC OPEN TO AMERICAN WAYS
AMERICAN	● AMERICAN CLOSED TO HISPANIC WAYS
	● AMERICAN OPEN TO HISPANIC WAYS

However, we eventually realized there was a fifth, quite fascinating stance that rises above the Hispanic/American quandary. It can be characterized by its break from cultural conditioning to assume a more integrated stance above its influences. This group waives being defined by either its Hispanic or American attributes and represents the ideal aspired to by all Hispanics.

DYNAMIC MODEL OF CULTURAL STANCES

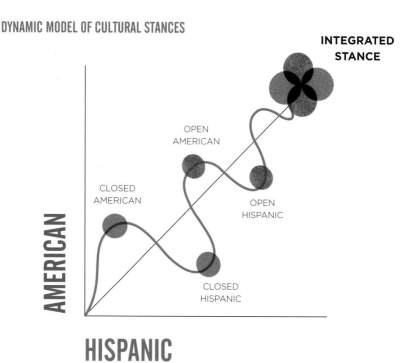

INTEGRATED STANCE

OPEN AMERICAN

CLOSED AMERICAN

OPEN HISPANIC

CLOSED HISPANIC

AMERICAN

HISPANIC

In portraying the five identity stances, we developed a dynamic model to explain how Hispanics' descriptions of themselves relate to a natural line that allows them enough flexibility to prevent being pigeonholed in compact, too tightly defined groups. As we have seen, the home countries avail themselves of elements from both cultures, hence, it would be erroneous to define the folks back home according to their affinity for one specific culture without taking into consideration their stance regarding the other.

Hispanics want brands to communicate with them in relation to the identity they've chosen. It's fine that, for convenience sake, we've agreed to lump all Hispanics into one segment, but we must recognize the differences within it if we want to achieve effective communication. It could well be possible that we're treating people that feel American and prefer to watch English-language TV as though they were Hispanics. Or perhaps we're addressing Hispanics that could care less about American culture. It's similar to the children's market. They want to be acknowledged as kids, while at the same time they want content or products to address them like pre-teens because that's the way they feel and define themselves.

FIVE IDENTITY STANCES

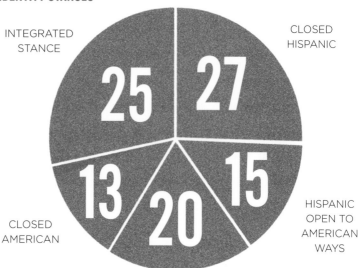

INTEGRATED STANCE

CLOSED HISPANIC

25

27

13

20

15

CLOSED AMERICAN

HISPANIC OPEN TO AMERICAN WAYS

AMERICAN OPEN TO HISPANIC WAYS

Each of the five stances has its needs and wishes. Nevertheless, they are all together in one ecosystem, which enhances them and fills them with meaning.

As seen above, our study shows that 27% of those surveyed hold to the Hispanic Closed to American Ways Stance, 15% are Hispanic Open to American Ways, 20% American Open to Hispanic ways, 13% American Closed to Hispanic ways, while 25% hold an Integrated Stance. For a better understanding of the inner workings of each of these segments, let's zoom in on what makes them different, what they need, how they relate to each other and how to get in touch with them and have meaning in their lives.

**HISPANIC CLOSED TO AMERICAN WAYS:
"IT WAS LIFE THAT BROUGHT ME HERE"**

This segment is made up of people who identify themselves as Hispanics or by the nationality of their country of origin, even though they live in the United States. This group has no desire to be linked with elements of American culture.

Fear and insecurity drive them. They seek calming, secure, basic stability at all costs. They would rather shop in Hispanic stores, where products and the language are familiar, than to venture out to American ones, where they hardly understand the codes. They tend to avoid conflicts, hence stick to their Hispanic networking groups. Their social groups are apt to be quite closed off, seldom accepting new people. Accordingly, they always adhere to a Hispanic social circle.

Spanish plays a major role in their lives because it is their first language, the one they read best and feel most comfortable speaking.

It's the language most used in the home.

Such is the case of a mother in Napa Valley, California, who didn't care to learn English because she felt it would be too hard. She's comfortable letting her American-born son be the interpreter whenever she gets into a pinch with the language. Every Thursday, when she and the son's godmother cook together, the latter reinforces her decision to not bother learning English, because, after all, they may return to the hometown some day, and life will get back to normal.

In fact, when we examined the photos we shot of Closed Hispanic Family homes, we discovered that most showed little signs of settling in, such as pictures on the wall or decorations. These Hispanics live on eternal standby, refusing to make their living quarters homey, in expectation of returning to the homeland, whether by deportation or their own decision.

Hence, their relationship with the United States is more strategic than ideological. They keep to the old country's cultural values and codes and hardly make allowances for local ones. A Closed to American Ways Hispanic father can be counted on to think it a bad idea to let his children study or live in another state when they turn 18, holding to the opinion that they should live at home until they marry.

The values that describe them are simplicity and devotion to family. They are one of the stances that in fact best exemplify the discourse of sacrifice, and all their undertakings go into reinforcing it. For the sake of emotional stability, this group's defense mechanism closes them off to American ways. They validate themselves by being as Hispanic as possible in the United States.

HISPANIC OPEN TO AMERICAN WAYS:
"IT ALL ADDS UP"

This category, composed of people who identify themselves as Hispanic or by the nationality of their country of origin, regardless of living in the U.S.A., is open to exploring and assimilating elements of American culture.

They are mainly motivated to connect with the American world without relinquishing the ways of the homeland. They enjoy exploring the novelties tendered by life in the U.S.A. and are apt to be flexible in their relationships with Americans. Although they hold their Hispanic values in high esteem, it doesn't bother them if their children go to college out of state, as long as they stay in close touch with the family.

Open Hispanics, similar to closed ones, are partial to using Spanish, because it's their first language, they read it better and it's the preferred language at home.

In contrast to Closed Hispanics, open ones feel quite a bit more comfortable with English, while still preferring Spanish when they have a choice.

In this sense, they're concerned about social belonging and actively seek ways to connect with their American communities. However, the values of the homeland are so important to them that they don't come to feel like Americans. They are more practical than Closed Hispanics in choosing which Hispanic customs to adhere to and easily drop them if they become a roadblock in their opening up to American ways. The same could be said for American values that interfere with Hispanic traditions.

An apt illustration is the Hispanic in Chicago who, beginning to feel more a part of the American community, moved his family into a predominantly Anglo neighborhood. His reason for doing so, besides establishing the roots he desired for his children, was to escape the pressures of the Hispanic world, which from his point of view, made it hard for him to get ahead. He relates that Hispanic *barrios*, where most of the people are closed to American ways, are commonly the ones that make it difficult to be open to cultures other than their own.

Nonetheless, his home is loaded with signs of homeland product consumption and Hispanic symbols. The man exuded Hispanic essence, yet felt it behooved him to open up to the United States. In fact, one of his sons married an Anglo woman. Naturally, Dad would have preferred a Hispanic woman (endowed with more feminine, maternal qualities, according to him), but he went along with it anyway.

They are Hispanics willing to settle down in the U.S. and seek ways to connect with the host culture so as to fulfill their desire to belong and explore new and different things. They validate themselves by being as flexible as a Hispanic living in the United States can possibly be.

AMERICAN CLOSED TO HISPANIC WAYS:
"WHAT DOESN'T HELP ME GETS IN MY WAY"

In this group, we find people who define themselves as American citizens, despite their Hispanic heritage. They prefer not to identify with the culture of the old country.

Similar to the Open Hispanics, they desire to belong to the American culture. However, as they feel threatened, they tend to go to extremes. They think the social structure takes issue with their being American, so they must validate themselves as such by all means possible, willing to go so far as to negate their Hispanic heritage. For instance, if they work as a bartender and somebody orders a drink in Spanish, they would feel so offended that they have to quash the desire to throw a punch. They don't like to be treated or acknowledged a priori as Hispanic, because they feel totally American and, furthermore, want to be addressed in English only.

Given their need to demonstrate how American they are, these folks become highly competitive and desire to excel at everything they do. Sidestepping Hispanic ways, they achieve higher levels of education and accumulate more wealth. They value competitiveness and success highly... the American way.

English is important to this group, preferring it because it's their first language and the one they feel most comfortable using.

This group's English is significantly better than their Spanish.

They are apt to feel their Hispanic heritage interferes and impacts negatively on their success, a pigeonhole for a group they no longer belong to. This situation is likely to trigger strong conflicts within the family, as they are seen as critics of Hispanic ways, maybe even as traitors who have rejected the values of their forefathers. To deny being Hispanic is often interpreted as abandonment of their parents, their culture, their values and beliefs.

This segment participates in Hispanic affairs only rarely and in private circumstances, as they are quite picky about aspects of their heritage they let into their lives. Women in this group, for instance, might enjoy occasionally cooking old-country dishes with their mothers, but would never encourage their daughters to learn. Perhaps they keep some memento from the old country, but stored away in a closet.

We found our exemplary Closed American in Los Angeles. Our after-dinner conversation included her mother and grandmother. The woman told us the best thing her parents ever did for her was to give her a first name in English, a counter to being saddled with a Spanish surname. For example, she opts to sign her letters and references with "Katy L." instead of her full name, Katy López.

These people take little interest in the traditions of their forebears and are much more comfortable identifying with and living as Americans. Their validation comes from being as American as possible.

AMERICAN OPEN TO HISPANIC WAYS: "MY PAST IS A FOUNDATION FOR BUILDING, NOT A BURDEN"

People in this group define themselves as American citizens, notwithstanding their Hispanic heritage. They are, however, open to relating with cultural elements from the old country while not neglecting the American ones that root them in the United States.

Thus, just like Open Hispanics, Open Americans seek to affirm their place in American society while remaining open to relating with the Hispanic community and their families. Their relationship with Hispanic culture is founded on a personal strategy aimed at keeping the family ties strong. Alongside their American identity, they enhance their lives with Hispanic aspects that are in concert with their families' values and beliefs.

Unlike Closed Americans, Open Americans feel equally comfortable with Spanish or English.

Their mother tongue is Spanish.

They are less able with English than Closed Americans, but their Spanish is much better.

An Open American woman in Miami told us she usually watched TV shows about health or interior decoration but every once in a while checked out the Hispanic soap operas so as to have something to talk about with the family and to brush up on her Spanish.

They advantageously use their Hispanic heritage as a tool to help them stand out. For instance, for them, Hispanic symbols play a part in personal stories that feature them as people outside the usual mold. Maybe their tables are graced with Talavera ceramic ware or the walls are decorated with Peruvian weavings (even if the family is Argentine!). For them, their Hispanic heritage is a big plus, affording them a distinctive identity they feel is more attractive and sexier than run-of-the-mill American. They make Hispanic heritage meaningful within the American context, but far beyond the stereotypical.

Their desire and willingness to conciliate would probably lead them to root for the old country's national soccer team were it to play against the U.S. team in the World Cup. They might even feel a soft spot for the land of their forebears, even though they've never been there. If they do pay a visit, It's apt to be to a tourist destination, Cancún, for instance. Curiously, on that basis, many of them construct an idealized image of Latin American culture: magical, glamorous, different.

In these folks' hands, Hispanic attributes become reinterpreted so that they worthily contribute to American life.

Their validation comes from assigning meaning and worth to Hispanic culture in the United States.

INTEGRATED:
"EVERYBODY HAS THEIR REASONS"

The persons comprising this segment build their identity from a birds-eye view of the cultures they live amongst, which is not to imply they fuse them. What they build is the ideal aspired to by all the other stances.

Having escaped the quandaries of the other stances, this group is perhaps the most complex. As we pointed out, they decline to be defined as either Hispanic or American and carry on life without either one conditioning or affecting their existence. In fact, their ability to soar above the cultural dilemma affords them a stance that's quite liberating and attractive for the rest.

We met the exemplary Integrated Stance person in Houston. He told us how important it was for him that his children learn to communicate fluently in Spanish, not only due to their heritage but because of the personal enhancement that learning another language bestows, be it French, Mandarin, Italian or whatever.

People in this group are equally at ease with English or Spanish.

In contrast to other segments, integrated homes significantly speak both English and Spanish.

This segment dominates English significantly better than the others.

People who take this stance explain they built their individuality based on their own personality traits and accomplishments more than anything that had to do with their cultural heritage. As a matter of fact, they are attracted to multicultural integration discourses where their tolerance and openness can shine.

They strongly desire to bequeath to their children an identity that can be built upon freely, liberated from cultural conditioning and complexes. Accordingly, they foster respect for values such as freedom and culture in the home. They might even feel superior to other Hispanics who've not attained such freedom.

These are people who learned to contextualize the cultural dilemma, validating themselves by rising above the problem.

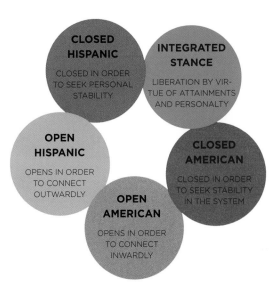

The stances we describe are broad sketches from stories Hispanics tell about their lives in the United States. With this script, they make decisions and relate to brands, products and categories. In turn, they give us an ideal excuse to strike up a conversation with them, as they suggest an identity conflict our brands can help resolve or at least diminish.

HIGHLIGHTS

In order to deal with the context, Hispanics need to take a stand on identity

They decide for themselves which of the two cultures they most identify with, and on that basis they strike a stance as either Hispanic or American, regardless of birthplace

They assume a degree of openness toward the culture opposite the one of their choosing and thus favor or limit influence from American or Hispanic culture.

There are five identity stances: **Hispanic Closed to American Ways**, **Hispanic Open to American Ways**, **American Closed to Hispanic Ways**, **American Open to Hispanic Ways** and the **Integrated Stance**

The **Integrated Stance** demonstrates the identity-posture ideal for the other four, as its construction exhibits a detachment from the cultural dilemma and the use of other elements unconditioned by its limitations

The stances could be likened to the eyeglasses Hispanics use to view and understand the world

PRACTICAL GUIDE TO THE STANCES

	CLOSED HISPANIC	OPEN HISPANIC	CLOSED AMERICAN	OPEN AMERICAN	INTEGRATED STANCE
LANGUAGE	Passive admiration of English	Active admiration of English	Spanish devalued	Both languages valued	Both languages valued
FAMILY	Family overly valued	Family flexibility	Forebears devalued	Family conciliation	Transmit multicultural values
VALUES	Simplicity and sacrifice	Flexibility and generosity	Competition and success	Conciliation and integration	Liberty and culture
HERITAGE	Respect and religion	Reinterpretation	Negation	Recovery	Contextual-ized

chapter 7

Up to now, we've seen that Hispanics make up a heterogeneous group, segmented in relation to their identity stances. If it seems odd that we should be addressing them by specific segments, just remember, tensions and conflicts exist in all groups. As we've seen all along in this book, all Hispanics feel the need to validate themselves and to make worthwhile the sacrifices of those who came to the United States seeking a better life.

They live under constant tension and hunt for ways to successfully go through the validation process by whatever means are at hand. One tool that's within their grasp, as we've pointed out, are brands of consumer goods. Tension is such that Hispanos welcome brands that acknowledge their conflict, that understand it, are involved in it and, as much as possible, aid in resolving it. They empathetically want the conflict to be addressed head-on, even dramatized or done with irony.

The way we use the term "conflict" shouldn't be interpreted in a negative sense, as though referring to a troubled teenager. On the contrary, it has to do with the kind of tension that's key to making any story (life or brand, for that matter) interesting and worthwhile to recount and to experience. It would be pointless to create strategies targeted at this market segment (or to write this book) if Hispanic stories were bereft of tension and conflict.

Hispanics have lived long enough in the United States to have accumulated material aplenty for a great story. The problem is, up until now they've had the feeling they're the only ones interested in telling it like they've experienced it. As there is a dearth of storytellers who can tell it like it really is, exceptional opportunities await the brands that gather up the story and capitalize on it. A brand that shows a thoroughgoing knowledge and comprehension of the Hispanic conflict stands a much better chance of becoming relevant than one that doesn't or, worse still, one that presents a false conflict.

All too often, strategies aimed at Hispanics sidestep the conflict as though it were discomfiting to refer to it or didn't exist at all. But we find the key for communicating with this market in our ability to go straight to what hurts and heal it by means of a dramatic solution. Stories, in other words. If we tell them their story, we become highly prized pieces in their game. It's like a person who, after suffering a tremendous loss, obtains solace by reading a book that relates a similar story.

In this sense, and keeping in mind the validation conflict common to Hispanics, it should be noted that the undertaking should aim for a concrete change; a transformation. Validation for Hispanics goes beyond becoming a valued member of society to encompass a shift that allows them to feel comfortable in their shoes. As in any story, the protagonist must undergo some sort of transformation (whether for good or ill) so that overcoming the conflict obtains meaning.

We have identified two avenues for Hispanics to seek validation: one, perhaps the more obvious, has to do with being rewarded for the sacrifices. But beyond imbuing the sacrifice with meaning, it must become materialized. It's that moment when a third-generation grandchild graduates as a physician from a top-ranked medical school or when a mother lands a part-time teaching job that pays well and leaves her plenty of time to take care of her children.

Usually, this sacrifice seeks the positive transformation of an entire family or its individual members. It entails the heroic role of persons who have attained greater ascendancy by means of an exchange. The sacrifice is neither idealistic nor unrealistic but aims to render benefits in ordinary life, evidence that their decision to come to the United States was worthwhile. It's a transition in which the first generation, the parents, desire to see the pay-off of their efforts in their children and grandchildren. Thus, in both senses, there is an overriding necessity and emotional pressure to make this transformation real. And your brand can aid or assist in making this happen.

The second validation avenue isn't exclusive of the other. This one has to do with the ability of Hispanics to transform themselves, to make the sacrifice worthwhile, and, in addition, contribute added value to the United States. It is a mechanism with which they seek to enrich American culture by vent of their own Hispanic attributes. This particular exercise in validation, though difficult, involves a reinterpretation of Hispanic heritage in order to transfer it with enhanced value and meaning to the United States. It's when a second-generation Hispanic listens to reggaeton instead of accordion bands or a third-generation youngster opens an up-scale taco restaurant or a second-generation young lady walks into a retro bar sporting a Peruvian purse and turns all heads.

Assigning new significance to Hispanic attributes shows their ability to reinvent codes to make them complementary to the United States. It's a creative way to imbue their story with meaning and differentiate themselves out in the world. It signifies even more, though, because customs and traditions gain new life when they gain new meanings. Although they had to undergo transformation to do so, they've become contextualized and made worthy in different surroundings.

Reassigning significance keeps Hispanic origins and heritage alive. It's like the chap with his reggaeton: he's still in the Latino groove, but a contemporary, hip-hop version.

Although reassigning significance is more common among the second generation onward, it's not unusual to find first-generation folks involved, as well. One clear example is how their expectations change in regard to products imported from Latin America. It seldom pleases them to find home-country brands in the same packaging. They'd rather see these products undergo a transformation similar to their own.

Q: How do I approach using the validation conflict in my communication?

A: One of the tones most utilized by Hispanics when talking about themselves, and one that could be of profit to a brand, is irony, understood as a message that communicates two opposing things at once. It could be a resource employed to involve the audience and get conversation going, because in provoking a free interpretation, it presupposes the public's cooperation.

They would like some of their codes to be reassigned so that a product's Hispanic attributes make sense in the United States and, furthermore, comply with its standards.

In this light, it doesn't matter which of the two validation avenues your brand might undertake in developing its Hispanic strategy. Whatever the choice, though, the role to be assumed is as an ally, a helpmate for Hispanics in their search for that validation. Seen from a narrative perspective, the roles of the characters in a brand's story must always be oriented toward what's outlined in the following chart.

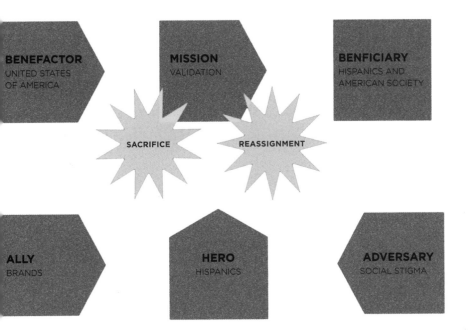

It's easy to give in to the temptation to cast our brand as the hero of the story, the one who's got everything under control, whose amazing powers bestow validation on the Hispanic. Warning! Do not fall into that trap! Instead, give the Hispanic the chance to decide how to use the brand. Let's imagine, for instance, a first-generation mother who's supposed to take dessert to a small event at her son's school. She's terrified because she only knows how to make Mexican *buñuelos* (deep-fried flour tortillas dusted with sugar) and she's afraid of giving the other moms the impression of a poorly adapted Hispanic family. But, *voilà!* She remembers there's an easy recipe for a classic American pie on the wrapper of the butter she just bought. She makes the pie, puts it on a pretty platter she picked up on the last trip to Oaxaca and takes it to the event, where everybody raves about how beautiful it looks and how great it tastes.

As you probably noticed, the brand of butter made no effort to show or tell that its recipe enabled the Hispanic mother to validate herself. It simply implied in an eye-wink to Hispanics and an alluring appeal to any American woman to buy the brand. All the while, though, it's performing as a helpmate for validation. Here we see a brand that knows its place is implicitly stated with its recipe, offering a solution for its target without forcing it to make a definitive choice between what's Hispanic and what's American. With this in mind, no matter a brand's approach with this market, it should always be aware that its role is to be the accomplice, indirectly showing its allegiance by depicting itself as a helpmate in smoothing out the conflict.

By now, it's likely some will be asking what happens with the brands that definitely do not want to enter into these validation narratives or, due to its category's nature, has no place in matters of culture. In these instances there is a highly desirable avenue that is certain to get a great deal of attention in the coming years: the search for autonomy above the cultural morass. As we've seen, just as the Integrated Stance segment looks highly attractive to the rest of the groups by virtue of its having risen above the identity and culture conflicts, brands liberated from the dilemma have a similar allure.

This does not mean to turn a blind eye to Hispanic tension and pretend it doesn't exist. Quite the contrary, it implies the hard road that leads to creating strategies or communicating messages that rise above the dilemma. As a matter of fact, to do it, we've got to talk about it. Otherwise, it might seem like we just skipped it. Beyond the American/Hispanic identity game, these folks long for discourses that allow them to build an individuality liberated from the culture context. Neutral discourses that embrace values instead of cultures afford them the opportunity to place their own personal stamp above any context.

This means that there's also an avenue for brands to exit out of the cultural dilemma, which enables individuals to construct beyond their origin or heritage. Moreover, it could free brands (in some cases) from overly segmented strategies. That is, if the brand or service has the credentials to step aside from the culture issue and, in this case, build upon premises and values unrelated to Hispanic tension. It's needful to also know if a brand has a Hispanic identity, either in origin or usage. Perhaps there are brands of detergents that would like to leave the dilemma behind but are unable to do so because they are products for a particularly Hispanic hygiene practice.

Whatever the case, we must know whether the Hispanic narrative conditioned by the validation conflict represents a major opportunity of approach for a brand, product or service. It's the task of each one to assess to what extent their brand or product is involved in this problem and can help to resolve it. Meanwhile, the tension and the Lego identity building we've been describing is a point of departure for a more thoroughly engaged and pertinent presence with Hispanics.

We've outlined five easy golden steps to keep in mind when creating strategies for the Hispanic market:

1. Be mindful of place of origin: assess whether your brand is free of place-of-origin conditioners (too Hispanic, too American, maybe even too multicultural). From there, figure out if you want to get in on the Hispanic game via cultural strategies or if you'd rather sidestep these conditioners and make your pitch on the grounds of other attributes, sticking with your brand's already established added value or differentiation.

2. Get rid of bad habits: figure out if you've been communicating with Hispanics solely along the lines of homeland values and missing out on other possibilities or approaches that build more value for this market.

3. Steer clear of stereotyping: ask yourself if you've recurred to stereotyping Hispanics in your approach to them, whether condescendingly or by simplifying Hispanic values. In other word, have you been too literal?

4. Find where you stand on the *Hispanometer*: ask to what extent some of your symbols appeal directly or indirectly to Hispanics:

ASK YOURSELF	OBSERVE
MY CATEGORY Do Hispanic attributes matter in this category or not?	In each of these instances:
MY BRAND Do I have symbols that connote Hispanic attributes or do I seem too American or multicultural?	**PRACTICAL LINK** Everything that's related to the way a brand, product or service is used. This has to do with specific Hispanic customs in its use.
MY COMPETITORS Do they use Hispanic elements to stand out? Do these detract from being competitive?	**CONFLICT** Pinpoint which conflict your product is likely to resolve. It's quite relevant that you distinguish whether this is a conflict of validation oriented toward giving worth to a sacrifice or toward reassigning meaning to a tradition. Check whether you are outside these conflicts or if you require a more autonomous discourse that rises above the culture dilemmas.
MY PRODUCT Does it have any truly intrinsic Hispanic values? Does its Hispanic attributes work in its favor or against it?	**CONVERSATION** What conversational means enable you to resolve the conflict (communication, activations, promotions, services, attention, etc.).

5. Whether to simplify or become more complex: find out to what extent you need to simplify or become more thoroughgoing in your relationship with Hispanics.

FOR BRANDS WITH AMERICAN DNA, WHETHER BY CATEGORY, BRAND, PRODUCT OR ORIGIN	In Latino cultures, what is said is not nearly as important as how it is said. Often the manner contains more clues and information than the message itself. Try to get to deep levels of what being Hispanic means: when they say "family," it doesn't necessarily mean what it seems.
FOR BRANDS OR SERVICES HISPANIC DNA, WHETHER BY CATEGORY, BRAND PRODUCT OR ORIGIN	Hispanics in the United States have learned the language of American brands (direct and to the point), its symbols and its messages. They expect to be addressed as Hispanics living in the United States. Accordingly, they want simple, clear and not overly saturated branding.
	Be sure to simplify your codes and recognize that a Hispanic living in the United States is not the same as a Latin American living in the home country: a Mexican living in Mexico is not the same as the one living in Chicago.

In the final analysis, though, all that we've covered in this book is just a mere inkling of the numerous possibilities of approach to the Hispanic market. The intent here is to afford a foundation upon which to construct a thoroughgoing conversation that rises above simple culture differences, especially when the aim is to become a real solution to a generalized conflict. Hispanics have established the rules of their game and have taken a stance, one that influences their consumer decisions every day. It is within our grasp to acknowledge them, understand the rules of their game and figure out to what extent we are willing to play by them.